The LOVE of HOME

The LOVE of HOME

INTERIORS FOR BEAUTY, BALANCE, AND BELONGING

KATE MARKER

Gibbs Smith

CONTENTS

———

INTRODUCTION

I've found that people often overlook the most basic yet most crucial question when it comes to their home: *Do you love it?* Do you love your home? Miss it when you're gone? Can't wait to get back to it? Do you feel joy and pride and purpose when you get to introduce it to others? If these questions sound like they could be about a loved one—your spouse, child, or significant other—that's the point. I believe that our *relationship* with our home is one of the most important ones we have. It's foundational, essential to a good frame of mind, to a good life. And just like any good relationship, it takes investment, thoughtfulness, and care for it to become mutually beneficial—that is, for your home to love you back.

As a professional interior designer who has worked with a myriad of clients across the country for more than twenty years, I know how to transform any space into something aesthetically beautiful and functional. But, honestly, that's not what matters most to me, and it's not what led me to this path. Growing up in a small town in the '80s, I didn't even know that interior design was a *thing*. All I knew was that I was a girl who loved art, had a secret superpower in math, and wanted to help people, and I had no idea how all those things could go together. Maybe it was seeing my mom as a teacher for all those years that planted the seed, but I just always knew that I was meant to connect with people, to find out what they needed, and to help them get there. When I finally had that aha moment midway through college that interior design could be my career path, it was so apparent to me that it was what I was meant to do that I left the university where I was pursuing an art degree, went straight to interior design school, and never looked back.

In the years since, I've discovered that my true passion is helping people turn their house into their *home*. What's the difference? A house is simply a structure. A home is where you know that you *belong*—that intangible welcome, connection, comfort, sense of being known and held—and your people do too. If your home is pretty but it doesn't serve your household in real life, if it doesn't speak to your personal story, if it isn't true to what you find meaningful, then it will never feel like it is truly yours. And I don't want anyone to miss out on that magic. That's why I do what I do.

Through these pages I want to show you how to cultivate a sense of belonging in your home by bringing beauty and balance—highs and lows, old and new, vintage and inexpensive—together. And I want to help you explore your own story and understand how your home is a part of it.

With every design principle demystified (I promise, paint color and patterns don't have to be scary!) and every visual story shared—from my clients' projects and my own home—my hope is that you will grow in confidence about your own good instincts to create a home that you truly love and that loves you back. Not a fling but a love that grows and changes . . . and lasts.

> My hope is that you will grow in confidence about your own good instincts to create a home that you truly love and that loves you back.
> —Kate

Beauty

It's an age-old question: How can we define something as subjective, as deeply personal, as beauty? For me, beauty is found in the way something—whatever form or color or style or shape it may take—touches you. Encountering beauty is an experience that floods us with feelings of awe and wonder and delight. And that's why in these pages I'll ask you many times and in many different ways how you want to *feel* in your home. What I'm really asking is what kind of *experience* are you wanting to create and cultivate in this space that exists solely for you and yours? And that's what's so thrilling about this work as a designer—getting to discover what feels uniquely beautiful or speaks to each client and their household and then curating and incorporating those elements—those colors, patterns, and textures, materials and art, and distinct pieces of their story—into their home so that their daily rhythms intersect with scenes that bring them quiet joy.

Here's the thing: You, like my beloved clients, already know what *feels* beautiful to you. You know the ambiances, atmospheres, and scenes from the natural world and your own history that bring you the most comfort or simply make you feel *good*. You may just need someone to help draw *out* that inner knowing and then give you some tips and tools for the journey. The next four chapters will help you explore some of those questions while building confidence—and the permission to call in creative support—along the way.

Embracing beauty in our homes is about being open to discovery as well as honoring what's already there—whether that's enhancing the good bones of an old house or weaving a family's personality and priorities into a new build. Cultivating lasting beauty in our homes and all the little pockets of our lives doesn't come from trends, nor does it happen all at once. It's a joyful, patient journey, one built on authenticity and staying true to your own version of a haven, whatever that may look like.

CHAPTER 1

OPEN TO POSSIBILITY

In the hustle and bustle of everyday life, the rush in and out of the door with the laptop or kids or groceries in tow, it can be easy to ignore what's been right in front of us—the wall color that has never felt quite right, the formal dining room that never gets used, the little '90s-era guest bathroom off the hall that always feels a little depressing because it's never been updated to our own tastes or style. We'll get to it one day. We can "live with it," right? Yet I've seen how these "misalignments" in a home environment affect the way people feel in, relate to, and use or *don't use* the rooms in their home on a daily basis.

I can't tell you how many clients I've had who bought a home and then never reimagined the layout, colors, purposes of a room, or furniture staging after the realtor pulled the For Sale sign out of the front yard. Years later, everything is still styled or laid out like a generic real estate template, even if that means certain spaces don't match the family's needs or regular activities. Put another way, they never made the home *theirs*.

Deciding to redesign your home isn't about keeping up with trends. It's about creating a home atmosphere that is an extension of you and your family, aligned with your needs, values, desires, and the kind of beauty that lights *you* up.

This chapter is an invitation for you to pause and rediscover your own home—to reexamine or even redefine the story you and your family want to live out within it. It's time to ask the questions that will help you begin to make your home *yours*.

DEFINE YOUR HOME'S FUNCTIONS

To gain a fresh perspective on what your household really needs and wants from your home, try this:

TAKE A STEP BACK AND LOOK AT THE BIG PICTURE. What parts of your lifestyle are in line with your values, goals, and dreams, and what changes do you need to make?

MAKE A LIST OF ACTIVITIES THAT TAKE PLACE IN EACH ROOM OF YOUR HOME. From lunch prep to office work to music practice to movie night, and so forth.

DETERMINE WHAT WORKS AND WHAT DOESN'T WORK IN EACH ROOM FOR YOUR HOUSEHOLD'S DAILY OR WEEKLY RHYTHM. Ask yourself what you need in each space to support the kind of lifestyle you want to lead. If you're a coffee lover, creating a corner with all of your fixings and cute containers for beans, sugar, and pods could add a boost to your day in more ways than one. If you have a house full of kiddos, a space with individual bins to wrangle their separate sports and school gear might be a necessity for a smoother start and end to the daily shuffle.

SPACES THAT DON'T GET ENOUGH USE. Could the underused space be reoutfitted and repurposed for a different function? A dining room that is only used on formal occasions could double as a lounge for weeknight family conversations or weekend gatherings.

ENTERTAIN A WISH LIST. What would you choose to have space for in your home if you could? A family office, a she-den, a cocktail lounge, a little library?

Creating a built-in with a rounded frame not only allowed us to draw from the softness of the arched doorways we added to the original architecture of the house but, with the addition of this charming woven cabinet, we transformed an area that previously felt flat into one of my favorite moments in our home.

DISCOVER YOUR OWN DESIGN INSTINCTS

You already know the kind of beauty you're drawn to, with or without labeling your "style."

When it comes to the interior of their homes, people tend to get overwhelmed about design because they immediately focus on what they don't know. *Is my style minimalist, modern, traditional, Bohemian . . . ?* Guess what. You don't need a design term to define the style that makes you feel at home. Focus, instead, on what you do know.

What are your very favorite places—the spaces that make you feel so good just to be there? Is it a favorite vacation destination, a special scene from your childhood, or a nature trail you love to stroll? Picture, in detail, one of those spots where you feel most at peace, comforted, or inspired. What are the colors, textures, and patterns that surround you?

When sitting with a client as we began planning the redesign of her home, she insisted that she wanted "the wow factor" to be evident in her house style choices. She kept repeating that phrase, convinced that "the wow factor" was what she wanted to see and experience in her home. But when I asked her to describe one of her favorite places to be, she immediately identified the spa area of a specific retreat center she visits—the exact opposite of the dramatic styling she thought she wanted. When she paused to examine what kind of environment and aesthetics

actually made her feel most at peace, the most herself, it was the serene, calm, almost earthy quality of that spa. So those were the characteristics we incorporated into the redesign of her home, and she couldn't have been more pleased (and relieved) with the results.

Once you more closely consider the places you most love to be, you may discover similar characteristics between them. Perhaps it is natural light that draws you in, or a cozy and intimate feel, or a certain spot that seems to have a magnetic pull, an ability to gather those you love. Now you're on your way to understanding your design tastes. From here, and before beginning any home project, I always encourage my clients to begin noting and "collecting" their preferences. (Creating Pinterest boards, categorized by specific themes or different spaces in your home, is a great way to do this.)

IDENTIFY YOUR FAVORITE COLORS, PATTERNS, AND TEXTURES in the places you feel like your best, most content and inspired self.

PAY ATTENTION TO WHAT VISUALLY DRAWS YOU IN, what catches your eye, in the world around you, whether it's a piece of art, a photograph, a home decor item, or even a piece of clothing.

CONSIDER YOUR WARDROBE. What outfits make you feel confident and happy? Is there a style of clothing or accessory that you feel great wearing? Take note of the elements that make up your favorite outfits and see if you can identify any patterns or consistencies. One of my clients only wears white, creams, and blues. If you pay a visit to her home, the palette of its interior is made up of the same hues. She simply feels her best—and most at home—in those colors.

LOOK FOR INSPIRATION in interior design magazines, on designer websites, and via social media platforms.

CONSIDER THE MOOD YOU WANT TO CREATE IN EACH ROOM, whether that is calm and relaxing, lively and engaging, or the like.

EMBRACE THE ASPIRATIONAL. When you see a style outside of your comfort zone that speaks to you, that lights a little spark of wonder or curiosity, experiment with it. At the very least, save the idea and come back to it and see if it still resonates. It may just be one of the risks you'll take in your project that ends up bringing you the most joy and satisfaction.

.

One of the best ways to keep the design process joyful . . . is to celebrate the little wins all along the way.

TRUST YOURSELF, TRUST THE PROCESS

The first time someone really commits to a home design project, they are inevitably surprised by how emotional the process can turn out to be. So many highs and lows—and yes, sometimes tears (though I'm a true believer that this process can and should also be *fun* all along the way). No matter how free-spirited, risk-averse, or anything in between you may be, *everyone* goes through emotional and mental phases in the process of transforming their home environment. Considering how intimate and personal our relationship is to our home, doesn't that make sense? Navigating change always stirs up feelings and questions, but if you know what to expect and how to build in support along the way, it becomes much easier to keep your eyes on the endgame—a home atmosphere you absolutely adore.

Here's what you can expect to experience (and a few tips to keep you steady and moving forward) as you begin to reimagine and redesign spaces in your home:

1. **EXCITEMENT** from the possibility of creating something new and unique.

2. **UNCERTAINTY AND CONFUSION.** As the process moves forward, the number of choices to be made can become overwhelming. Decision fatigue can set in as you try to distill countless options and define some kind of style framework, causing you to feel hesitant and unsure of your vision.

> *Antidote: Identify your team before you begin.*
> Whether you hire a professional designer or call on a family member or friend with a good eye who wants the best for you and tells you the truth, identify a small core team who will understand your vision and hold it up when things get blurry and you start to feel shaky.

TIP: GO BACK AND REVISIT THOSE ASPIRATIONAL PINTEREST BOARDS YOU MADE. REMIND YOURSELF VISUALLY OF WHAT YOU'RE WORKING TOWARD.

---

3. **FRUSTRATION.** Design is an iterative process that involves multiple rounds of feedback and revisions. When you're trying out ideas, some things you think will really work in a space just don't materialize as you imagined. It's easy to get frustrated with the back-and-forth nature of the process.

*Antidote: Keep perspective and
embrace the art of editing.*
Remind yourself that trial and error is a neces-
sary part of the journey. You can take my word
for it—some of the "mistakes"
made in the middle of the process turn
out to be the most beautiful features or
elements of the design in the end.

4. **DOUBT AND FEAR** can creep in as you begin to
   question your decisions, leading to insecurity and
   the temptation to avoid risk altogether.

   *Antidote: Lean on your team for reassurance
   to get your project through to the next step.*
   It's one of my mantras because it's been true
   with every client I've ever served: **When
   trust happens, beautiful things happen**.

TIP: MAYBE DON'T PULL THE MOST OPINIONATED FAMILY
MEMBER OR NEIGHBOR IN TO OFFER FEEDBACK JUST YET.

---

5. **TRUST.** When you rely on your team through the disillusioning patches and begin
   to witness some wins, you'll gain confidence in your ability to make your creative
   vision a reality and your home design will gain momentum.

6. **SATISFACTION.** You're going to walk into your home and experience a new sense of
   pride in it. It'll feel so good that you'll be bursting to share it with others.

It was truly a joyful design process for me and my team to transform this rental bedroom into Townie Cottage, a haven of tranquility, where guests can escape, unwind, and truly relax.

OPPOSITE: To make the cottage a serene retreat for visitors, we brought in touches of nature, an abundance of texture, and layers of design details mixed with the cozy comforts of home.

CELEBRATE EVERY WIN

One of the best ways to keep the design process joyful—as it should be; you're creating your own haven, after all—is to celebrate the little wins all along the way: the drawer pull that captures your fondness for texture, the statement plants that convey your love of nature, or an unexpected paint color that brings in a feeling of joy or a touch of surprise. Stop to appreciate every new layer and step. Find the wonder. Give a high-five to your team. Revel in what a gift it is to get to create something beautiful.

CHAPTER 2

BUILDING ON GOOD BONES

As a homebuyer, you will inevitably have things you love and *don't love* about any house you acquire. (And I would dare to say this applies to those who've built their own homes too—things never turn out *exactly* as you imagine them on paper.) Maybe you adore the architectural style of the house you purchased but dislike that there's scant storage or a funky traffic flow. Maybe you bought the house because it was close to your child's school but you have a *meh* feeling about its aesthetics. Wherever you fall on the spectrum, there's one key tip that can help you bring your home more in line with how you want to experience it . . . and help you fall more in love with it as a result: get curious about the backstory of your home.

Restoring the original stucco texture of my former 1920s Italianate, crafted by Italian artisans one hundred years ago, was a labor of love that was completely worth it.

DO A LITTLE DETECTIVE WORK

DO YOU KNOW YOUR HOME'S ARCHITECTURAL STYLE? Maybe it's mid-century modern with clean lines and a minimalist feel. Maybe it's some version of a Craftsman with a simple silhouette and a great front porch. Or a Victorian with ornate woodwork, a gabled roofline, and a little tower or turret.

WHEN WAS YOUR HOME BUILT? What was happening culturally in your area or even in the nation during that time period?

WHO OWNED THE HOUSE BEFORE YOU? How many owners has it had over the years and what can you find out about their stories?

In much the same way that investing in a personal relationship—asking thoughtful questions to get to know someone better—brings two people closer, getting curious about your home's backstory will help you understand it better, endear it to you, and make your investments in it all the more effective and worthwhile. Knowing a little bit about the history of your home—its existing story—can help you build off its strengths and work with—instead of against—its best features.

Allow the appreciation of the history of the home to be highlighted but not necessarily dictate the style. And if you feel your home doesn't have a distinct architectural leaning, embrace the opportunity to treat it as a blank slate. You can create your own new look and a sense of the style (or styles) that appeal most to you—that character and personality— whether through big changes or small but powerful design details (check out chapter 7).

HOME STORY: KATE'S ITALIANATE

When my family and I first knew that we wanted to live in the house we would call home for several sweet years, our attraction to it didn't have much to do with the building itself, at least not at first. It was the beauty of the land and nature around the house that drew us in, the charm of the ducks and geese on the lake at the back of the property. It didn't hurt that on our first visit down the driveway just to peek through the windows, there was a perfect sunset making everything around us glow. While the hundred-year-old structure obviously had character to spare, I didn't begin falling for the house until I started digging into its story. As I asked around, I learned that the architectural style is called Italianate and that there

were only two previous owners of the home, each family having lived there for at least fifty years. The most recent owners told me about how back in the early 1900s when the house was new, a little boy would draw water for the carriage horses out of a spigot underneath the stairs and how another boy would blow a trumpet from the landing, announcing the arrival of guests before they headed downstairs to the small ballroom. These incredible anecdotes sold me on my own house. And they sold my family on it too. I've overheard my daughters retelling parts of the house's history to their friends or other guests, and that just thrills me because it became a part of their story too.

Embracing the abundance of texture original to the family room, we brightened the river rock with a mortar wash and refreshed the weathered wooden ceiling beam with several coats of white paint.

Making just a few tweaks to this existing built-in, such as adding lights and updating shelving brackets, transformed it from dated to modern and fresh while still preserving its initial charm.

LEFT: When we bought the Italianate, this sunroom, despite its magical wooded lakeside views, felt heavy and cold. However, by refining the shiny, original bluestone floors to a raw, more natural state, selecting brighter furniture, and introducing a funky yet striking rattan light fixture, the space now radiates the bright warmth for which it was always intended.

ABOVE: Adding a restored limestone sink and tadelakt plaster walls brought the storied feel on this old home's stucco exterior right into this moody little powder room.

While the hand-plastered crown molding around the ceiling of this family room (above) and dining room (opposite) wasn't a style I would typically choose, I wanted to honor the true craftsmanship it represents. Brightening and lightening the paint color made the molding work with the home's modernized features while still honoring the original artistry and history of the home.

Cabinets in "Dark Olive" from Benjamin Moore and terracotta-framed, green-patterned tile from Kate Marker Home gave this spacious kitchen an earthy tone that aligns beautifully with its nature-filled window views.

To make the addition of a new breezeway and garage look cohesive with the old home structure (left) we added vertical cedar planking to the family room of the old structure and carried it through the additions, topping the new garage with the same cedar shake roof.

FIND THE GOOD BONES

Identify the unique qualities, those original elements, that give your house its character. Does it have built-in bookcases, a telephone nook, artisan millwork, or fireplace shelving? What has been covered up by outdated trends over time? Maybe there's beautiful hardwood under that shag carpet. Uncovering the beauty that is already in your home is a fundamental part of restoring your home's integrity, bringing it back into alignment with the best version of itself. A home with good bones coupled with thoughtful design can provide comfort, functionality, and value for today and generations to come.

Lots of bright white, accented with light parchment colors from the floors to leather chair backs and drawers made this kitchen feel like a true celebration of the homeowners strong Swedish roots.

PRACTICE THE ART OF THE *EDIT*

I love using the term *edit* when redesigning a home, because editing something inherently means that not everything needs to change. (Such a freeing realization that makes any project feel more doable!) When you edit— whether it's with words in a book or features in a home—you home in on what's already good and build on that. Of course, on the flipside, you identify what's not working and needs to be changed.

Note the structural elements of your house, such as the layout, size of the rooms, the

windows, the materials used in construction, and the placement of the rooms and their features. All these things can influence how comfortable your home is to live in and how appealing it is for others to visit. How can these foundational elements of the home better serve the daily rhythm of your household or your lifestyle? If your kitchen doesn't open to your dining room or living room, for example, and that floor-plan flow is important to how you spend time with your family around mealtimes, creating that connection between spaces may be a design priority for you.

REVISIT YOUR WHY

Even if there are very few things you like about the aesthetic of the house you purchased, there's a reason you bought it. What was it? Why are you in this home? Maybe it wasn't about the structure at all; maybe you love the natural scene behind your home—a pond, a field, or a big grove of trees. If so, focus on building out and enhancing the windows that frame the view. Maybe the exterior of the home really appealed to you, but the interior doesn't speak to you at all. Consider incorporating some of those exterior design elements (stone, brick, timber, or metalwork) on the inside of your home to bring in the texture and ambience. Maybe you purchased that house (sight unseen?) solely to be close to your child's school and part of that community. Prioritizing the development of welcoming and connective spaces in your home for family and school-friend gatherings might win your heart over to the purpose of why you're in this home and give you some inspiration with working with whatever house "bones" you have. Whatever the reason you find yourself in your current home, getting curious about your house's story as well as determining the house's strongest features and where they connect with your reasons for choosing it will help you prioritize your resources, time, and energy. It will allow you to focus on the areas that can make the biggest impact for your household—bringing your home's story and your family's story together in a way that enriches both.

Prior to purchasing this one-hundred-year-old home, I wasn't familiar with Italianate architecture. However, learning the story of this place down to the spigot where a carriage boy would get water for the horses of visitors won over my heart and stirred up a passion to ensure that any new design work would honor its beautiful old bones.

CHAPTER 3

DON'T STRESS ABOUT PAINT

I see it with every single home project, with every friend or client: By far the most common source of anxiety among homeowners during (or even before) a design project is actually the most flexible and fixable part of the process: picking paint colors. Time and again, clients will get caught up in fear of making the wrong choices, uncertainty around matching colors, pressure to conform to color trends, or worry about the investment of time and money if they change their minds. But here's the freeing reality of it: paint is actually the *easiest* and *least expensive thing to change* when designing a home. I promise. So take a breath and focus on the big picture first.

START WITH EVOKING A MOOD

Part of what trips up people is they tend to start by asking, *What color should I paint this room?* But this question offers no helpful parameters, compass, or true north. Instead, asking, *What do I want this room to feel like?* provides a goal that can much more easily be achieved. Maybe you grew up in a big family where cooking and family meals are happy memories and you want your kitchen to feel light and open, nostalgic to your family roots. Perhaps you'd take comfort in a study where you feel tucked away and secluded, a place for intense focus, what I call "a moody little office?" Is there a special built-in or nook in your home that you want to highlight in an imaginative way, showcasing the house's personality and yours?

Before you start to think through paint colors, ask yourself what story you want a room to tell and hold, how you and your family members want to feel in a certain space. Once you've determined that, you can think about the colors that bring out those emotions in you and make a fitting match.

CONSIDER WHAT COLORS MEAN TO YOU

You can find a plethora of resources that are meant to tell you what a certain color symbolizes ("red means passion, yellow is happiness," etc.) and plenty of studies on how different colors affect our brains. But I'm much more interested in asking what various colors mean to *you* specifically. I've found that how each person experiences color can be very different according to their personal history and makeup. What color makes you feel most inspired? Ask yourself why. Does a certain color have a negative association?

I had a client from Belgium who had tons of spunk and personality and loved incorporating color throughout her home, but she absolutely did not want to use any green in her remodel. She shared with me that green reminded her of growing up in Europe where the weather was always gray and rainy while the plants and grass were vividly green. Green made her feel down, like something was always out of reach. A few years later, I had another client who was the polar opposite in color association: The *only* color besides light neutrals that she wanted to incorporate in her home was—you guessed it—green. So much so that my design team dubbed her our #LivingTheGreenClient. (Get it? Living the dream? Our team has too much fun with this.)

HOME STORY:
#LIVINGTHEGREENCLIENT

For my #LivingTheGreenClient, a fervent yogi, green makes her feel alive and grounded at the same time, in touch with growth and change. She is a highly successful businesswoman in a corporate role, and having green accents in her home makes her feel nurtured and closer to nature at the workday's end, even while indoors.

OPPOSITE: A long hall in "Dark Olive" from
Benjamin Moore showcases the beauty of using
molding with color to finish out and ground a
space.

Little touches of green throughout the home
serve as constant connections to the natural world
without oversaturating airy spaces.

DON'T STRESS ABOUT PAINT

KATE'S TRIED-AND-TRUE HUES

While I hope you feel energized and empowered to experiment with any colors that express what you want to feel in a space—get going with sample swatches!—I know it helps to have a solid place to start. The following whites, lights, and darks are the foundational paint colors I keep coming back to time and again, and here's why.

White & Lights

Stepping into spaces with lots of white and neutral tones can feel easier to breathe in and open to possibility, and they also provide a perfect canvas for layering in pops of any color or pieces with interesting texture. But it can be a challenge to find whites and lighter paint colors that have no funky undertones and look beautiful in all different lighting environments. Here are some of my favorites that always deliver.

"OXFORD WHITE"
BY BENJAMIN MOORE
Closest to a true white—bright, crisp, and great for projects with a modern appeal. I used this color on the exterior of my Italianate-style home to freshen it up to today's more modern look.

"SIMPLY WHITE"
BY BENJAMIN MOORE
Strikes the perfect balance of being a fresh, bright white without being harsh. It's my favorite trim color yet is equally beautiful on walls in nearly any room.

"WHITE DOVE"
BY BENJAMIN MOORE
Creamier and warmer than "Simply White," perfect for spaces that have a generous amount of natural light (shown throughout our #TwoEyesOnDesignClient).

"SWISS COFFEE"
BY BENJAMIN MOORE
Cozies up a space with touches of gray and cream and is less reflective than other whites, making it a natural choice for a vintage space. I used this color not only in my hundred-year-old home but in an abundance of client projects too.

"CLASSIC GRAY"
BY BENJAMIN MOORE[†]
Offers just a whisper of color and is one of the best combinations of soft gray and warm white in one. I especially love this one cut to 75 percent as it lightens the taupe-y white even a bit more.

"CITY LOFT"
BY SHERWIN-WILLIAMS
Welcoming and muted, a pale taupe gray that is especially wonderful on kitchen cabinets (shown in #NiceandNeatClient).

Before you start to think through paint colors, ask yourself what story you want a room to tell and hold, how you and your family members want to feel in a certain space.

The rafters, beams, and a tongue-and-groove planking lent so much architectural interest and texture to the twelve-foot ceiling of this breakfast room that a seamless sweep of Benjamin Moore's "Swiss Coffee" from the walls upward felt like the right kind of bright.

DON'T STRESS ABOUT PAINT

A Moody Blue & Darker Hues

For darker colors, I'm drawn to deep grays, dense hues of navy and inky blues, and a variety of greens. I love how dark color can ground and define a space in the best way, making the people in it feel a little more "held" too. And there's more diversity in this grouping than you may think, as the same paint color can present in a completely different way depending on hardware, light fixtures, the light exposure in the room, and art pairings.

"WROUGHT IRON"
BY BENJAMIN MOORE
Makes a stunning backdrop for gold, brass, or polished nickel hardware; it feels very classic but with a touch of green blue.

"KENDALL CHARCOAL"
BY BENJAMIN MOORE
Brings a smooth yet approachable sophistication to any space. This is a great charcoal with a hint of brown to it.

"MANOR HOUSE GRAY"
BY FARROW & BALL
Evokes beautiful shades of grays and greens and pairs seamlessly with bolder darks or subtle lights (shown in our #BlendedandBlessedClient's kitchen).

"STUDIO GREEN"
BY FARROW & BALL
Yields a refined yet earthy essence, especially wonderful for pensive rooms or spaces (shown in our #PicturePerfectClient).

"DOWN PIPE"
BY FARROW & BALL
Presents differently in every setting, making it mysterious and a "most asked about" gray paint color from my followers and clients (#TwoEyesonDesignClient pantry/mudroom).

"HALE NAVY"
BY BENJAMIN MOORE
Pairs well with nearly anything—so versatile that I consider it a neutral. Just a good ole classic true navy (shown in our #beautifulinside-andoutclient's mudroom, #ItsElectricClient's mudroom).

DON'T FORGET:
PAINT IS NOT THE ONLY WAY TO BRING IN COLOR

It's easy to take for granted how much color you can bring into your home through means other than paint. Neutral walls and cabinets provide the perfect backdrop to layer in satisfying sprinkles of color throughout the home via furniture, bed linens, pillows, plants, art, accessories, and more. Added perk: many of these items are easy to change out for seasonal celebrations or evolving tastes, helping to keep things fresh. We often bring in green through live plants to make a space feel like we are bringing in the outdoors.

I love a good vintage rug for adding color too. The best part of incorporating a vintage rug is how it tells its own story through its pattern, age, and geographic origin.

Art is certainly the most expected way to bring in color, but depending on the space and what other colors are already happening, art that offers a tone-on-tone effect—rather than being a standout showstopper in the room—can help a space feel more complete and cohesive.

DON'T STRESS ABOUT PAINT

Benjamin Moore's "Kendall Charcoal" on these breakfast nook built-ins creates a sweet contrast with the white interiors and white oak shelving.

Farrow & Ball's "Down Pipe" takes on a dark blue-green hue in this pantry,
setting off the space nicely from the bright, white oak kitchen that lies adjacent.

CHAPTER 4

PATTERN &
TEXTURE CAN
BE FRIENDS

Perhaps second only to the perceived stress of picking paint colors, the idea of combining patterns and textures in a given area of the home tends to intimidate people. They're afraid there will be "too much going on" in that space. We've all witnessed rooms where design elements have gotten wild and out of whack (read *unbalanced*), but I'm here to demystify the process because layering patterns and textures really can and should be one of the more fun and rewarding parts of dressing a room. After all, patterns and textures speak to so many of our senses. Textures add visual and tactile comfort, character, and warmth. Patterns can bring in playfulness, intrigue, and sophistication. They light up the mathematical and artsy sides of our brains at once, which makes us feel a little more engaged and alive to our surroundings. When well-placed and working together, combinations of pattern and texture are what make our spaces feel complete and full in the best ways.

KNOW (AND PLAY WITH) THE RULES

Playing with patterns and textures isn't as complicated as you might think. But it's a lot more fun if you know a couple rules to the game:

1. Keep scale in mind for balance.

A basic understanding of scale—how the size of the pattern on one element in a space relates to the size of the pattern on another element in the space, as well as the size of the space itself—is your winning ticket when it comes to choosing patterns that will work together instead of compete. An easy rule of thumb is to pair large- and small-scale patterns together rather than large with large or vice versa. For example, if you're using wallpaper in a space where you have a patterned rug or tile flooring, just make sure that one of the two features a large-scale pattern and the other is small scale. See the balance?

When it comes to how a pattern relates to the size of the space around it, think about the following scenario as an example: If I'm laying a diamond-pattern tile in a foyer with a modest eight-foot ceiling, a twelve-by-twelve-inch tile pattern might work well. But in a house with a lofty foyer boasting a twenty-foot ceiling, the smaller pattern on the floor would feel dwarfed in comparison, while a twenty-four-by-twenty-four-inch floor tile pattern would probably feel just right. That's the way the scale works—whether you have a trained eye or not, you can sense when the scale is off in a room because the effect feels chaotic rather than cohesive, haphazard rather than grounded.

PATTERN & TEXTURE CAN BE FRIENDS

2. Build pattern and texture layers from the ground up.

If you didn't pick up on it yet, I tend to start building layers of pattern and texture in a space at the literal foundation, which means beginning with whatever needs to happen with the floor. A beautiful, patterned rug can be so satisfying to build a room around. And if a neutral rug is the right foundation for a room, it's still one of the most impactful ways to bring texture (think high pile, a smooth weave, knobby, plush—you name it) and warmth to any space. Gah, I just love great rugs—can you tell? (An exception to this rule would be when a client has a special art, textile, or furniture piece they already know they want to design a room around.)

Even wood flooring can hold its own magic as a pleasing textural foundation in a space. Reclaimed wood tells its own story in the grooves, nicks, and imperfections that translate as character and add rich depth to a home. And whether reclaimed or newly milled, the natural texture of white oak, red oak, or walnut can be highlighted with the thoughtful application of oils or stains. The best part? Wood floors wear beautifully over time, slowly creating their own distinct patinas with every footfall.

PATTERN & TEXTURE CAN BE FRIENDS

THERE'S ALWAYS A PLACE FOR PATTERNED TEXTILES

Once you've got your foundation down, choosing the textiles for a space is where the play in "pattern play" really gets fun. Whether your style is bold or refined, patterned textiles can be used to add interest and depth to a room through larger elements (window treatments, breakfast-nook banquettes, comforters, armchairs) all the way down to little details, like a tiny sconce shade. And who can forget all the throw pillows, maybe the easiest method of all for breaking up or adding contrast to a neutral space, especially when you know the following trick for mastering the perfect patterned-pillow combo.

My go-to throw-pillow mix always incorporates some form of stripe, a floral pattern, and a geometric pattern. Because they'll be nestled right next to each other, don't forget the trick to maintain balance so the patterns are complementary: large scale with small scale. If the floral pillow has a large-scale pattern, the geometric-style pillow should feature a small-scale pattern. Tie them all together with the stripe as your neutral, and voilà! *chef's kiss.*

Sometimes texture itself can manifest as a pattern. Bouclé is a great choice for adding both pattern and texture at once because it delivers a high-sensory touch.

STONE

AD at 100

BETTER WITH TIME: USE LIVING MATERIALS TO REVEAL PERFECTLY IMPERFECT PATINAS

I rarely use hardware with coated finishes in a home, and that applies to plumbing hardware, cabinet pulls, light fixtures, and even stairwells. There's just something so beautiful about how living materials, like unlacquered brass, copper, or marble countertops, age naturally with use—it can't be matched in manufacturing. The unpolished surfaces—exposed to air, water, the oils on our hands—develop their own beautifully imperfect textures with time that seem to say, *Life is happening here. This is more than a house—it's a home*. Using elements in the home that gain patina can be a subtle way to add texture to pattern. I adore the effect of an unlacquered brass faucet in a powder room against the backdrop of a cool, patterned tile wall. You may not consciously notice the contrast; you just know it feels so *right*. And that's what it's all about.

From a comfort-zone mindset, people tend to think all the hardware finishes in one room need to match each other. But that approach can be very limiting when it comes to creating spaces that have creative depth and balance. Sure, all your plumbing fixtures in a bathroom should be the same material (unlacquered brass is my undisputed favorite there), but that doesn't mean that you couldn't use a different finish or material on the cabinet hardware or mirror. Real style, in my opinion, is made up of all the little details that bring beauty and function, patinas and polishes, patterns and neutrals *together* in whatever way works best and feels truest to you. That sentiment is what one of my most endearing clients always called "the right fit" when we remodeled her family's home from the studs out.

PATTERN & TEXTURE CAN BE FRIENDS

LEFT: An unlacquered brass faucet and range that will patina and tarnish in time give a living quality to this kitchen. Adding an oil-rubbed bronze hood and the vintage feel of reeded glass cabinet doors ensures that this kitchen will only gain more warmth and character through the years.

ABOVE: As long as all the plumbing fixtures match, mixing metals or the "jewelry" in a space is a beautiful way to add depth as seen in this timeless primary bathroom, which features a polished nickel faucet and unlacquered brass hardware and light fixtures.

HOME STORY: #THERIGHTFITCLIENT

"We trust you. Just do whatever feels like the right fit for us."
That is hands down the dreamiest thing you could ever say to an
interior designer, and it was the constant refrain #TheRightFitClient
used every time we discussed another space or detail in the remaking of their 1920s Cape Cod–style home. Their complete trust
and that creative license not only made me want to create a more
timeless, cozy, beautiful, and functional
family home than they could have
imagined for themselves but it also set
me free to build in all the layers of wonderful textures and patterns to accomplish just that.

**When trust
happens, beautiful
things happen.**

OPPOSITE: Layers of high texture can take an entryway, like this one, from a pass-through to a full-on moment worth pausing over.

RIGHT: Smooth millwork paneling topped by the woven look of grasscloth paper and edged by an airy, patterned drapery creates a perfect trifecta of feels.

OPPOSITE: Adding pattern and color (Benjamin Moore's "Sabre Gray," to be exact) to the wall behind a high-texture cane bed grounds this primary bedroom and gives every element from the heavily contrasted ceiling and raffia-wrapped light fixture down to the chunky, black bedside lamps a sense of place.

PATTERN & TEXTURE CAN BE FRIENDS

Pattern and texture come in endless forms and work together in just as many layers and configurations. The trick is to find the spots where it feels most meaningful in a space, whether the edge of a mirror, the pulls on a bathroom vanity, the paper or millwork or tiling on a wall, or simply woven baskets for storage.

Balance

When it comes to creating a home that we can fully use and enjoy, beauty without function is, honestly, just vanity. The last thing I ever want to hear from a client is that a space we've created together is "just too beautiful to use." You should be able to sink into every room in your own home with more confidence and ease than anywhere else on the planet. It's yours, after all. Balance, in form and function, is what allows a home to be both livable and harmonious.

When a space is out of balance, it doesn't require a degree in design to sense it—you know something is off even if you can't put your finger on exactly what. And no matter how subtle the sense of unease, disproportion throws our ability to be fully at rest in a space, to feel held. Symmetry is certainly foundational to balance, but asymmetry, when thoughtfully employed, can be wonderful for our senses too. The juxtaposition of contrasting neighboring elements—textured and smooth, old and new—create design moments in a space that pique our interest and inspire us. Thoughtfully reserved open or "negative" space, free of elements and items, can be just as impactful as a statement. And sometimes the littlest details—a special finish, a curved edge, a sentimental item in a special spot—can pack the biggest punch of all.

In the next few chapters, I'll show you how the components of a room, from large to small, can live and work together, play off one another. Because while achieving balance may not always be the most noticeable part of good design, it's the supportive backbone behind a space that is not only beautiful but nurturing too. It tells your subconscious: all is well, working together as it should be, in a space that is meant just for you and yours.

CHAPTER 5

EVERYTHING IN THE RIGHT PLACE

et's dive into a topic that may not seem the most exciting at first glance: balance and function. While it might not have the immediate allure of other design elements, such as color or texture, it holds a crucial place in creating spaces that truly resonate with us. Let's explore how balance brings harmony and functionality to our homes, making them not just aesthetically pleasing, but also nurturing environments where we can thrive.

HOME STORY:
#HALLWAYTOHEAVENCLIENT

How do you make a house with twenty-foot-tall ceilings feel like a home with warmth instead of the Taj Mahal? This was our (incredibly fun) challenge with our #HallwayToHeavenClient (named, in part, for having the most gorgeous and enormously long and tallest hallway ever). The answer lies in creating balance through the thoughtful placement of elements throughout each space: not simply left to right but also above and below.

RIGHT: Adding this built-in, floor-to-ceiling wall mirror with an antiqued, smokey finish was our secret sauce for making a very large, open room feel warmer and less cavernous.

OPPOSITE: Vertical planning is just as important as horizontal when it comes to design. These crazy-long white drape panels lend a sense of space in a two-story tall room, framing a super shiny piano that feels grounded atop a highly textured rug.

An arched doorway softens a highly symmetrical hallway leading to a powder room, and the architectural brass light fixture is the perfect contrasting cherry, or star, on top.

SYMMETRY IS
ALWAYS IN STYLE

Everyone knows that architects and designers love symmetry, but I want to talk about why achieving symmetry in the spaces of your home matters to *you*, even if you may not know it yet. Whether we recognize it consciously or not, we're naturally drawn to symmetry. Imagine drawing a line down the center of your body; your very makeup is symmetrical. We see it every day in each other and in the mirror. We build on it: matching earrings in either ear. We alter it too, just for fun: a bracelet or cuff on this wrist but not the other.

It's the same in home design, no matter your style. Even if you're creating a really funky contemporary space, you'll always go back to symmetry to make it work. You might achieve it a little differently than you would in a traditional home, but symmetry is still the key to creating the balanced background that we all crave.

So what is symmetry in the design of a room? It's the feeling that the elements of a space are equal or in correct proportion to one other. It's the sense that components of a room hold the same "weight" on either side—one side or portion of a space doesn't tip the scale as too heavy or too light when you take in the full scene.

When all the elements that make up a room are in the right place, your eyes can move throughout a space without getting "stuck" on something. There's an ease and a flow to the space that you really don't or (shouldn't have to) notice in the day-to-day . . . unless it's not there.

IF NOT SYMMETRICAL,
MAKE IT INTENTIONAL

Achieving balance in a space doesn't mean that its two sides perfectly mirror each other. Sometimes that's not desirable, and often it's not possible. There are plenty of oddly shaped and bulky elements in a home—not to mention doorways—of which we only have and need one (take large kitchen appliances, for example) in the home. Unless you're a live-music venue with dueling pianos, you're unlikely to have matching grand pianos in the same room, right? But a well-placed light fixture that draws the eye up over that one bottom-heavy piano and a rug with lots of texture and warmth beneath it to offset the shiny coldness of the piano's shellacked exterior can make all the difference. In the end, it's all about helping our minds be at rest by sensing that the components of a room are working together.

NEGATIVE SPACE IS A (HUGE) POSITIVE

A nonnegotiable part of capturing a healthy sense of balance in your home is making sure there's enough negative space (i.e., space *sans* stuff) in every area of your home. Whether you're viewing a room, a built-in, shelving, a portrait gallery, or even the fireplace mantel, your eyes should be able to easily flow and travel through the space—they should know where to go. If the visible path is confusing, you know there's too much happening.

If you find it difficult to determine if a room in your house is overly cluttered (I get it—we all love our stuff, right?), maybe it's time to bring in some fresh eyes and perspective. Don't be afraid to ask a trusted friend or neighbor who

has a good design eye to help you identify the spots that feel overcrowded. I don't make these choices alone either. The team of designers working with me and I all have different opinions to bring to the table on whether an accessory or a piece of furniture or art is working in a space or feels like too much.

The beauty of negative space is that it gives you the chance to actually notice and appreciate what *is* there. When things are crammed together, you can't appreciate shapes or unique items . . . everything blurs together.

An overly cluttered view saps energy and focus even if subconsciously. So much of the home's role is to provide a space for rest and restoration, the ultimate place of comfort and safety. And holding space for . . . well . . . *space* helps us breathe a little easier.

MILLWORK DETAILS CAN WORK MAGIC

When it comes to truly creating a space for *every little thing*, millwork tricks of the trade are where it's at. The following subtle fixes are just a few examples of how my team and I bring function and beauty together behind the scenes—a winning combination every time.

◊ Instead of visible continuous drill holes (to position shelving) down the sides of a built-in, my team and I have developed a special little panel that can be placed inside the built-in so that it looks beautiful from every angle.

◊ Admittedly I'm not the biggest fan of glass shelves—maybe they're just a little too contemporary for my tastes—but if I put a light at the top of a built-in, I want that light to shine all the way through the piece. So I've taken to lining the front of the shelf in wood, so what you see is a wooden shelf, but then leaving glass on the back portion of the shelves so that the light comes through beautifully all the way down and throughout the built-in.

◊ Lining the front edge of a kitchen trash pullout with a strip of metal—I typically use brass, stainless steel, or iron—not only keeps this highly used item from wearing down as quickly (not to mention easier to clean and thus more sanitary) but it looks beautiful too. Now, every time you do something as mundane as toss a piece of trash, you'll get a happy little glimpse of this gorgeous piece of metal at the top of your drawer.

◊ A desk with a small brass-framed grommet hole built into the top offers a sleek way to hide cords from laptops, monitors, and other electronic devices. Nightstand drawers with cutouts at the back allow you to charge your phone at night while tucking away surface clutter (not to mention distraction from sleep).

Creative, functional solutions that provide the "right place" for elements in our homes really do affect how we live in and feel about them. Achieving balance doesn't always mean going big. Often it's hidden in the little details.

CHAPTER 6

THIS MAGIC MOMENT

It never gets old—those involuntary *oohs* or *ahhs* that spring from people when they encounter a striking design moment in your home, a scene that surprises and delights their senses. The whole point of creating the "wow factor," after all, is the joy of sharing it. Sometimes, yes, that awe can be stirred up by a piece of art so stunning that it's hard to look away from it or some fabulously unique light fixture hanging low over a table. Don't we all love a good conversation piece? But just as inspiring to me is the slow-burn, more subdued kind of magic we can create by combining design components in interesting ways.

The high contrast of black drapery rods and window mullions framing white art on a white wall and warmed by the layer of camel leather chairs from Kate Marker Home all comes together to create a subtle, but striking visual.

LAYER ON THE IMPACT

In a recent project, I hung a textured but completely white piece of art on a white wall. It was pretty but maybe not something to pause over. Sometimes adding an art light over a wall piece can make all the difference, so we installed a small antique-y brass number over this austere white painting. All of a sudden, there it was: a gorgeous little moment that could hold your gaze, brought to life by simply bringing those two contrasting elements of warm brass and the bright white together.

So much of moment-making in design is like that—finding complements and layering elements that either make each other standout—old and new, rough and smooth—or become a whole new thing when brought together. Slightly overlapping pieces of art resting on a mantel, for example, can make a bigger impact than propping up one piece alone.

HOME STORY:
#THIRDTIMESACHARMCLIENTS

We say it so often that it's become a mantra around our office: *When trust happens, beautiful things happen.* Our #ThirdTimesACharmClient's a family we've worked with on three separate projects and built a relationship with for years—are living proof. When it comes to designing their spaces, they trust that our work together will result in magical design moments—from one end of their home to the other. Maybe that's what I love most about their latest project: it isn't about one grand scene or jaw-dropping entrance but seamless and subtler moments of inspiration all around. And isn't that what we want—to be continuously greeted by moments that make us feel a little more alive around every corner?

OPPOSITE TOP: Powerfully framing the transition between each room and drawing the eye through to the next space, these rustic, antique beams are the architectural moment in this home.

OPPOSITE BOTTOM: Even staircase landings can foster a feeling of wonder when you add thoughtful features like this rattan sideboard with glass-base lamps that illuminate (but don't obstruct) the view of this gorgeous staircase.

A gravel path leads to this stunning home entry where a
gas lantern on lime-washed brick crowns a portico over
charming glass doors that beckon all inside.

THIS MAGIC MOMENT

OPPOSITE: A traditional element in an uncommon spot, like this interior window situated between the butler's pantry and kitchen and framed by antique beams, makes the view even more special.

MAKE BIG MOMENTS IN SMALL SPACES

Don't overlook the small spaces when it comes to making an impression. I love to make a little guest bathroom into a moment—to pack in the interest, contrast, and special details in a spot that can so easily get overlooked. Designed mostly for guest use, powder rooms are the perfect place for homeowners to break out of their design-style comfort zones and try things just for fun: put up that wallpaper with the playful print, a cool wall tile, or maybe a funky mirror. The element of surprise, the unexpected pop of pizzazz—that's what's so fun about it, not only for guests as they experience your home but for you too.

The entryway is another area of the home packed with potential for creating an experience through design. As a guest's first impression of the home, the foyer or entryway is a terrific opportunity to share a glimpse of the style that will be shown through the home. A special artifact, an antique cabinet, a vintage rug, or something to show personality can do the trick. Fresh flowers or greens can always elevate any space, but they're especially impactful when they're one of the first scenes to greet you at the door.

Sometimes an extraordinary design moment is made around something ordinary, just in a reimagined shape or form. This circular window, wreathed with vines, draws the eye to it like a magical portal, which looks in on a special sunken office (pictured opposite).

If you love what you see through your windows, that outside view is (or can be!) a powerful part of how you and others experience beauty within your home.

FRAME THE VIEW

Often the things that fill us with the most awe aren't things we've had any hand in creating. An enormous ancient oak tree, an open field, a lake view, or simply a wall of green where the ivy, jasmine, or honeysuckle vines have completely taken over—there's no doubt that the wonder of the natural world holds the trump card in design. If you love what you see through your windows, that outside view is (or can be!) a powerful part of how you and others experience beauty within your home. Maybe you put in bigger windows or glass doors to optimize the view. Floor-to-ceiling windows can be showstoppers in and of themselves, and a simple window treatment can be a stunning finishing touch around almost any frame.

Don't worry—expensive, dated, and heavy drapery isn't your only option for framing a window, not by a long shot. It all goes back to whatever feeling you want to create in a space. A simple soft-white linen—my personal favorite for window treatments—is incredible for making a room feel cozy and complete without distracting from the real star of the show in the space, whatever that may be. On the other hand, in one of my edgier projects, we used a streamlined glazed black linen to frame windows against a black-and-white-checked wall to bring the drama. We loved the result, how the sheen of the glazed linen made the space chic and exciting at the same time.

However big or small, surprising or subdued the moment, what a gift it is to be able to create spaces in our homes that inspire us to live a little more creatively, to make a little more magic.

CHAPTER 7

THE POWER OF THE LITTLE DETAILS

While it's true that the placement of the larger elements in a room may make or break the balance, small touches can hold surprising sway over how a space actually feels. I like to think about the finishing details as the jewelry of a room—the polish and pizzazz that bring the whole outfit together. Far from trite, the small elements that make up the final layer of a space are often what brings its personality to life, what makes a house feel like a home that belongs to *you*.

LITTLE DETAILS CREATE BIG FEELS

You'll have to forgive me for the repetition, but even when it comes to finishing details, it's crucial to go back, once again, to that foundational question: *How do I want this particular space to feel?*

For a master bedroom where you're looking for serenity, for example, high-contrast details would be jarring—the wrong kind of energy. But dramatic touches might be just the ticket for that guest powder room where you want to create some interest and have a little fun. Maybe that's through whimsical wallpaper, a unique wall-mounted faucet, or a playful edge on the window treatment that makes it feel special. It really doesn't take much to set a whole mood, especially if a little detail holds big meaning for you.

I was recently reminded of that truth in a tender way with a client whose mother had passed away shortly before I helped her design her family's home. The client left all her decorative accessories with me and my team to incorporate into the family's spaces as we saw fit, without knowing any of the stories behind them. One of those pieces was a little brass-key sculpture that I styled on a coffee table in the sunroom, her favorite area of their home. When my client walked in later that day and saw the key on display, a big smile and big tears came simultaneously. "My mother gave me that little key," she told me. The simple act of seeing a little detail in its own special place in a room she adores touched her heart in a powerful way.

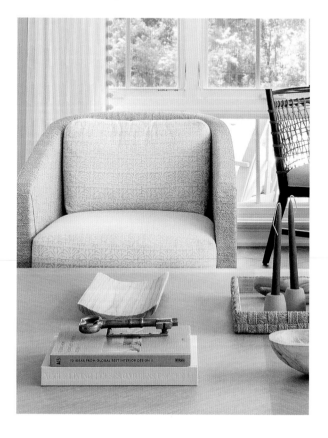

HOME STORY:
#DOWNTOEARTHCLIENT

Sometimes making a space feel more personal can come down a single strip of material. Yes, really. When my #DownToEarthClient approached us about designing the interior of their new, spacious English Modern–style home, they wanted to honor the architecture of the house while making the interior feel like a fitting backdrop for their laid-back personalities and warm hospitality. This family simply exudes authenticity and openhearted friendliness. And our challenge was to take a traditionally formal style and add the details that would make it feel just right for the most approachable couple and their two young children.

Using raw materials for the details in our design work felt key to make their home not only attractive but accessible and, yes, down-to-earth, just like they are. So we chose hardware and millwork finishes that would live with our clients and evolve alongside their family over the years. The simple brass strip we added between the white tile back-splash and marble countertop in the kitchen is a tiny feature, and yet it's one of my client's favorite details about her kitchen because it adds warmth and interest and that certain special touch. Her husband feels the same way about the exposed hardware and plumbing in the master bathroom, incorporated into a glass shower wall. Exterior brick on the floor of the family studio—a combined mudroom and arts-and-crafts space—is both appealing and grounding, setting the stage for kids and adults alike to be free and artsy, to make a creative mess without worry. Arched entryways between rooms draw a person into the next space and make them feel tucked in and filled up.

All together, the little things really do add up to a home that has not only beautiful bones but also a big heart.

Little design surprises are a delight to discover and rediscover in a home, like this simple brass strip in between white backsplash tiles that is reflected in other elements around the kitchen, such as the island apron, pendants, and cabinet hardware.

Incorporating exposed brass plumbing into this glass shower wall was one of those detail decisions that not only turned out visually stunning, but felt uniquely special to the homeowners, a couple who exudes approachability and authenticity, just like the feel of this space.

———————

Antique doors, modernized with new hardware, bring a comfortable, lived-in warmth to the landing of this new-construction home.

OPPOSITE: When we found this vintage chest in Round Top, Texas, I knew it could convert into a one-of-a kind vanity, perfect to offset a new countertop, bright tile, and shiny fixtures in a timeless way.

MIXING OLD & NEW
ELEMENTS MAKES MAGIC

There's a mysterious kind of synergy that happens when you bring old and new pieces together in a space. Maybe take that vintage cabinet that made you feel a certain kind of way when you came across it at the flea market and put it right next to a modern console table—and, somehow, both pieces pop in a whole new way. Or try hanging contemporary art over an antique chest. Mixing old and new works so well that once you start, you won't be able to stop yourself from looking for more opportunities to create that satisfying sense of juxtaposition. And why should you?

THE POWER OF THE LITTLE DETAILS

PLANTS BRING IN MORE THAN A BREATH OF FRESH AIR

Few things elevate the mood of a space like incorporating nature indoors through live plants. It's a juxtaposition that truly makes a difference for us as living beings, providing a balance between the vibrant, growing life and the static, inanimate elements of our homes. I always have at least one plant of some kind in every little space of the houses we design.

While it's hard to beat the literal freshness of real plants, for those with a self-proclaimed black thumb or for areas of a home lacking sufficient natural light to sustain live plants, impressively realistic-looking faux plants are available these days to still provide that splash of green where needed.

A few spots that are often overlooked when it comes to bringing spaces to life with flowers or greens:

MILLWORK—a faux plant can add a touch of green to an array of accessories.

NIGHTSTAND—a feel-good moment when you walk into the room or turn on the light.

KITCHEN—rosemary or lavender next to the range adds a romantic touch.

SIMPLE TRICKS OF THE TRADE CAN BRING BALANCE

You might be surprised at what kinds of things can ground a space that feels disproportionate. It could be as simple as choosing bun feet for the bottom of the bathroom vanity instead of wrapping it with a toe kick. Maybe it's adding a little scalloped detail to a powder-room mirror or the top of a cabinet that otherwise feels blah. And speaking of cabinetry that lacks personality, imagine this: a Shaker-style cabinet with tapered feet, painted a soft gray, with distinctive hardware and a woven handle. Suddenly the cabinet is pretty darn cute instead of basic, all because of the details.

One more cabinet tip: Because they often feel top-heavy, framing a wall-cabinet unit by adding a vertical panel that connects the cabinets to the edges of the open countertop and finishing with a stunning tile backsplash or even tongue-and-groove paneling behind the counter can ground the whole structure and make everything work together.

The little decorative details highlight the work you've already done in a space, creating more interest around those larger elements and pieces of furniture that make up the foundational structure.

DECORATIVE ACCESSORIES FILL OUT THE BIG PICTURE

Sometimes decor gets the rap of being the unnecessary extra in design. But I've found that without that final layer of curated accessories, a room feels unfinished. The little decorative details highlight the work you've already done in a space, creating more interest around those larger elements and pieces of furniture that make up the foundational structure. These final touches—baskets and trays, bone beads or carved wooden chains, bookends, bowls, small sculptures, artifacts and meaningful mementos, vases or planters, pillows and throws—help to complete a room's story, though maybe none quite as literally as a thoughtful selection of coffee table books. I like to incorporate one or two books, all beautifully bound or designed, that speak to your hobbies or interests—a beautiful volume on design, a book that explores or gives historical background on the area where you live, and so on.

When all the little details are working together, a space feels warmer—and warmth equals welcome.

Belonging

The greatest compliment I ever receive after designing a home for my clients is hearing them say, "It feels like us." Sure, they say, it has the signature KMI touch: it's cohesive, polished, fresh, inspiring . . . but somehow it feels personal too. When designing, what I really want to know is that, regardless of the architecture or design style at hand, the way we've designed a client's home makes them feel connected to it; they feel a deep sense of belonging within its walls. After all, isn't that what this creative work is all about?

A sense of belonging is born when beauty and balance are brought together in intentional, thoughtful ways. It's both a physical experience—the smells, sights, tastes, and textures that feel like home—and an inner reassurance. It's a subconscious, comforting knowing: *There is space for me here.* That's why I always want to make sure that the setup of a home prioritizes the activities and types of relaxation—from hobbies to family games nights to that first morning cup of coffee—a particular household enjoys most. I let those themes dictate the details in the big spaces for gathering all the way down to the tiny nooks for tucking away in needed alone time. I'm passionate about ensuring there's a place for everyone and what they love, but there's nothing I adore more than making sure there are also reminders of who they love or have been loved by woven into the details of their homes. You'll see some beautifully sweet and nostalgic examples in this last section of chapters ahead.

Nothing connects more powerfully than love. Design that incorporates symbols of that love—whether through a whole wall of framed sheet music that belonged to a beloved family musician or a small, sentimental token peeking out of a built-in—reminds us that we belong, not just to and within our homes but to each other.

CHAPTER 8

SPEAKING TO YOUR SENSES

Remember at the beginning of the book when I asked you to imagine the place you most love to be in the whole world and what makes you feel so good to be there? If you let yourself really relive those settings and scenarios in your mind, I bet that whatever's at play in creating the ambience you love is more than just what's visible to your eyes. It's your favorite place because of how your other senses are engaged too—the feel of the breeze off the coast or the softness of that chair in the perfect reading nook; the smell of pines from the porch or something wonderful baking in the oven; the sound of lively chatter around you at that café, moody music in the kitchen, or simply a peaceful stillness you can sink into. So much of design, of course, is visual. But for a house to truly feel like a home, it should speak to all your senses. And it can do that when we make some subtle but thoughtful choices in design along the way.

HOME STORY:
THE LEO COTTAGE

When my husband and I found our lakeside cottage in Michigan, the interior of the house looked nothing like I wanted it to, but everything else about it engaged our other senses in such a magical way that we were both completely taken with the place on our very first visit. Carefully tended garden beds, full of the colors of the season, led our way up the walk to the front door. We could hear the lake lapping on the shore. It may sound funny but as we stepped in the door, even the "old cottage smell" of the house hit me just right. It made me feel so cozy inside. The way we fell for that little cottage, even before all the pretty design aesthetics were in place, was such a great reminder to me that cultivating a sense of comfort and belonging in a home requires more than visual beauty alone.

Even the roofline of this cottage is quirky, lending this living room–turned-bedroom to a host of funky design choices, like a vintage footed bathtub right on the bedroom floor.

OPPOSITE BOTTOM: The cozy crackle of burning logs is almost palpable with just a glimpse at this charming woodstove and log holder perched mid-room, a picture of functional beauty.

LEFT: Because prioritizing organic elements in spaces creates a seamless connection to nature, we vaulted the ceilings and added rustic wood beams over a raw-edge wooden coffee table and wonderful, old Audoux-Minet chairs.

ABOVE: Even the vintage-inspired oven range design we selected communicates a simpler time in a cottage kitchen full of details that remind us we're in a place where we can choose to go slow.

SPEAKING TO YOUR SENSES

LET THERE BE (THE RIGHT KIND OF) LIGHT

Few things have more influence on setting the mood in a space than lighting. Today's LED lights last so much longer than incandescent bulbs and can give your space beautiful, natural-looking illumination rather than yellowy or fluorescent looks that used to be the only options. Thankfully there are more choices when it comes to overhead can lights now too.

Instead of the bulky six-inch recessed can lights that are so disruptive to the flow or millwork on a ceiling, there are now tiny two-inch recessed cans that come in round, rectangle, or even square shapes and provide the same amount of light as the old-style cans with a much smaller opening. I used to say can lights in a ceiling are like acne to a ceiling. We all must deal with overhead lighting decisions at some point or in some spaces—specifically in high-function areas like kitchens or family rooms—but the smaller the ceiling light fixture, the more unobtrusive they will be. The trick is to make sure you have a mix of light sources in every space. You may need can lights in the bathroom, specifically the shower, but you can use sconces over the vanity. Both beautiful and functional, sconces bring the light source down closer to your face.

In a living room, a dressy or cozy space meant for having conversations or reading books, you may not need overhead lights at all. Decorative lighting—pendants, sconces, art lights, and lamps—may be sufficient.

One of the things people tend to forget when designing a room is to put a floor outlet in the middle of a space, especially in a family room or any kind of sitting room where you'll want a console or table lamp, or a floor lamp between chairs. If you're building a new home, you'll want to consider the furniture layout early on so you can plan for any floor outlets to be placed under a sofa or chair instead of your lamp cords having to run all the way from a wall.

And don't forget to add a dimmer switch to your lighting sources. It's the simplest and most inexpensive way to easily adjust the mood and atmosphere of a room, from high-productivity to relaxing mode, from bright-day to soft-evening energy.

CREATE COMFORT THROUGH
TEXTILES AND TEXTURES

Every surface we touch in our homes—from the kitchen counters to furniture to towels and linens to the floorboards under our feet—sends little signals to our brains about how to feel. We're such tactile creatures.

But even simply viewing texture on elements we rarely actually touch, especially textiles, can make us feel a certain way. The material you choose for a space's window treatment, for example, can change the feel of a room from light and breezy (linen) to moody or sophisticated (wool).

Even the hardware on a window treatment has an effect. Most often I like to use a one-inch-thin wrought-iron rod, and I do a French return into the wall because I don't want the finial to be a factor in the design. But if I want a room to feel more traditional or woodsy and rustic, I might go with a chunkier rod or a heavier finish—a natural patina for that classic character or a shiny finish for a bit of glam.

Window treatments also give a vertical bearing to a space, taking your eyes from high to low. Mounting the drapery right under the molding on your ceiling, instead of just above the window, will make the room feel bigger.

DESIGN FOR WHAT YOU WANT
TO HEAR & WHAT YOU DON'T

Window treatments have another magic trick—they help to soak up noise so that it's not bouncing all over the place. In open floor plans especially, having enough furniture, drapery, or quality rugs to fill the space and absorb sound is key to avoiding an echo effect in your home or hearing every noise or movement from other members of the household. It's another reason why layering and finishing out a space—like adding a stair runner on clattery stairs—can make such a difference. When building a multilevel home, having your builder insulate between floors is a game changer when it comes to blocking sounds you don't want to hear and creating a snugger, more peaceful home atmosphere.

For sounds you *do* want to hear throughout the house, like great music, there is so much amazing technology now that allows for the high-quality sound to come in a more aesthetically pleasing setup. Instead of a large TV sound bar breaking up a beautiful design aesthetic on your wall, console, or mantle, for example, there are speakers that you place behind the drywall in your home. Maybe you want to add a speaker in the shower or where you get dressed. Thinking through the little details of your routine when planning sound technology is another small way to make your home the place you actually love to start and end the day.

SOAK UP EACH SEASON OF THE YEAR WITH SIMPLE SWITCH-OUTS

I love how the cycle of changing seasons in the natural world continually offers us something to anticipate in the days ahead. Whatever time of year is your favorite, there's something new and something nostalgic to experience in every season. Changing out design details inside our homes not only helps us savor each season more but it also keeps our homes feeling fresh, engaging, and, above all, super cozy. Seasonal colors can be brought inside with a variety of plants throughout the year. Pillows and throws can shift from breezier textiles in warmer months to cozier knits in cooler seasons and, of course, nostalgic patterns and tones for the holidays. Taking down December holiday decor can be an opportunity to think about what you want your home to feel like in the new year. While your pieces are already in transition, it could be the perfect time to choose fresh artwork or other decorative pieces or something different to put on your walls—or maybe just less.

EXPLORE SIGNATURE SCENTS THAT SMELL LIKE HOME

Our ability to smell is one of the most powerful senses we have when it comes to instantly conjuring up good memories and associations. Many potted plants offer sweet scents and can bring a bit of fresh air indoors. Even plants that are best grown outside can be brought in during the weeks that they're flowering and taken back out after the blooming season is over. Try temporarily bringing in rosemary, lavender, bay laurel or sweet laurel, orange jasmine, or a small potted citrus tree.

While scented candles may be one of the more obvious ways to usher in the ambience of a certain season or the holidays, I love when I see people claim a signature scent for their home—a fragrance that means something special to them or tells a little part of their story. A friend of mine wants her house to smell like there are chocolate chip cookies always baking in the oven. For her, the smell of freshly baked cookies is the most welcoming and comforting sensation you can get in a home, and she wants everyone who visits hers to feel that warmth.

Whatever details you add or routes you take to get there, the more your home engages your senses in ways that enrich your day-to-day, the more you'll feel at home in your own spaces and your guests will too.

CHAPTER 9

SLIP INTO YOUR COMFORT ZONE

O f anywhere on earth, our homes should be the places where we feel most at ease. That means feeling physically secure, of course, but also feeling comfortable enough in our spaces to let down mentally and emotionally—the reassurance to relax and be fully ourselves. We need spaces in our homes that inspire play and recreation, creativity in our work, rest or reflection—whatever we need most in the moment—without worry about the outside world. When it's time to head back to the office or wherever life takes us, a thoughtfully designed home is one we leave feeling refreshed and restored from the many ways it offers comfort.

Bringing the same rustic beams, classic staircase style, and flooring from upper levels down into this family's gaming room, elevated their basement into what I like to call a lower level.

OPPOSITE: With a comfy charcoal lounge sofa, big leather ottomans for propping feet or dealing cards, and a brass reading lamp, this stair landing was transformed into the favorite landing *place* for this household's kids and their friends.

DESIGN FOR DOING WHAT YOU LOVE

Prioritizing thoughtful spaces in your home for whatever brings you the most relaxation, rest, and enjoyment ensures that the activities that most enrich your life happen more often. Whether that's a spot to tuck away with a good book, enjoy game night with the family, watercolor by a window, or practice on the golf simulator—whatever your jam is, whatever gives you joy or simply a way to decompress, it's worth creating space for.

HOME STORY: #STEPPINGUPOURGAMECLIENT

When one of my clients, a dear friend, told me that she really wanted a special spot to drink her morning coffee and take in the view outside, we had already fully planned the design for her family's sunroom. No matter—her daily ritual was well worth pausing for and rethinking our layout. While I don't usually like to place furniture in corners, sometimes there's a great reason to break your own rules. We put a small, beautiful white-oak table in the corner of the sunroom with woven-back chairs and a view of the weeping willow trees at the edge of the pond on the back of their property. A soft window treatment with a whimsical pom-pom edge framed the view, and we finished off the moment with a little brass sconce over the table. For my friend, who lost her mother not long ago and held her memorial service under those same willows, that gentle space is more than a coffee nook—it's a place to pause every morning and reflect on good memories with her family and make plans for more in the days ahead. It's just a corner of her home, a relatively small space in comparison to everything else going on with the household. But because of the thoughtful way it was appointed and the intention behind it, my friend's little coffee-drinking spot is the space in her home where she most loves to be.

OPPOSITE: Adding an antique step stool to a butler's pantry might seem like a simple concession, but for my client, it's a detail that's made all the difference in how she feels about using the space. Now the pantry, with its dark-stained cabinets, and soapstone counters lit by a floor-to-ceiling window is more than beautiful; it's accessible too.

SLIP INTO YOUR COMFORT ZONE

Bardiglio-marble tumbled floor tile grounds this primary bathroom with a soaring ceiling, and is just the kind of wonderful texture you want underfoot in a space where feet are often bare.

CHOOSING DURABILITY
DOESN'T MEAN COMPROMISING ON DESIGN

The more forgiving the furniture and other materials are in our homes, the more relaxed and confident we can feel about using them. Whether you have small children or love to host and don't want to stress over spills, there are so many options now for designing with materials that can withstand heavy use and are easy to clean up but still look stunning. For one of my clients with a big family, counter stools with a high-quality vinyl seat that look just like leather but are a breeze to wipe clean after meals are the workhorse stars of their kitchen. Choosing a higher "double rub" count—the number of rubs a fabric can withstand before showing wear—for furniture fabric or upholstery will give your sofa and chairs a longer life. High-performance materials, such as polypropylene or wool, in rugs help them stand up better to cleaning. Even for marble countertops—that gorgeous but infamously porous material—you can invest in specialty sealers that completely prevent unwanted scratches and stains.

THOUGHTFUL FURNITURE PLACEMENT & PROPORTION LETS YOU SINK INTO THE MOMENT

Beyond the actual comfort of a sofa or chair, the distance between furniture pieces can make the difference for whether you or your guests are relaxed in a sitting area. The trick is to provide that subconscious confidence that everything you need is within reach. When you can't easily reach your drink from where you're sitting, for example, you have to reposition your body every time you want to take a sip. It may be a small adjustment each time, but it cuts into your or your guest's ability to be fully at ease or focused on whatever has your attention. Here are some good rules of thumb:

COFFEE AND SIDE TABLES. The standard distance to put between a sofa and coffee table is about eighteen inches, but sometimes that feels too far. I typically stick with fifteen to eighteen inches between the sofa and table. If you're using a round coffee table or ottoman, you may even want to push it to twelve inches. To ensure you don't have to reach down too far, the top of the table should come to the same height or within an inch of the height of the sofa or chair seat. For a side table, the top of the table should come within an inch or two of the height of the arm of the sofa. Simply put, you don't want to have to reach for whatever's on the table.

TIP (REGARDING WHITE SOFAS): I'VE WORKED WITH SO MANY CLIENTS WHO LOVE THE LOOK OF A WHITE SOFA BUT FEEL LIKE THAT'S NOT AN OPTION FOR THEIR FAMILY BECAUSE "IT'LL SHOW EVERY STAIN." THE TRUTH IS, WHITE SOFAS ARE ACTUALLY THE EASIEST TO CLEAN BECAUSE YOU DON'T HAVE TO WORRY ABOUT FADING COLORS IN THE FABRIC. SO IF YOU LOVE THE LOOK OF A WHITE SOFA, GO FOR IT! PLUS, YOU CAN ALSO BLEACH WHITE AND CLEAN STAINS EASILY, MAKING MAINTENANCE A BREEZE.

STOOLS AND COUNTERTOPS. Check to see if there's an apron extending below your kitchen countertop or dining-room table when choosing or placing your barstools and chairs, to ensure there's enough space for legs of all shapes and sizes to be comfortably seated there.

LIGHT FIXTURES AND DINING-ROOM TABLES. A dining room light fixture should never be wider than your table. No matter how great the meal, light shining in faces or on the floor instead of highlighting the table will throw off the ambience, for sure. I've found that choosing a fixture around two-thirds of the width of the table feels balanced.

TVS AND FIREPLACES. If at all possible, I try to avoid placing a television over the fireplace in a client's home. I get it—sometimes there's no other choice due to a room's layout or the need for symmetry, and there are lots of creative ways to hide the screen or make it look like art these days. If you're focused on symmetry, and positioning the TV over the fireplace is the best move, just make sure the placement isn't too high to where viewers from a low sofa have to crane their necks. (Not comfy or fun.) If you have the option to place the television in built-in shelving or even on a piece of furniture to the side of the fireplace, positioning a great piece art over the fireplace, often the center viewpoint of the room, rather than a TV can go a long way toward creating a more peaceful, connective-feeling space, one centered around people instead of programming.

The bottom line is that creating true comfort in the home—both physical and internal—is the apex of where function and aesthetics meet, where we can use all our spaces with confidence and convenience and still be inspired by their beauty.

CHAPTER 10

CONNECTION IS WHY WE'RE HERE

As much as I deeply believe in the value of cultivating inspiring beauty, bringing supportive balance and structure, awakening the senses, and creating comfort in our homes, none of these things are the ultimate goal in designing homes that we love in and of themselves. These design aspirations are simply the background for and pathway toward what matters most: connection to the people *in* your home—yourself and those you love. Authentic connection is one of the most vital ingredients in the recipe for belonging. It's the real *why* behind it all. Because connection to our homes and each other not only brings joy but it also adds meaning to our daily lives.

A few years ago, my two daughters, ages ten and eight at the time, and I sat down at the kitchen counter just for the joy of creating together. We took watercolor paints and brushes and spent a sunny morning painting swirls, stems, dots, and dashes in patterns that covered the art paper before us. Not long afterward, I took some of the artwork my girls created that morning and worked with vendors to produce textiles (and later tiles and wallpaper) featuring some of those patterns. I wanted to share a visual piece of my family's story with others in their homes through these offerings and incorporate the special designs into my house too. Now every time my husband, my girls, and I see those precious patterns in the material of the banquette and on the tiles of the kitchen backsplash, it's a sweet and continual reminder that we're connected to this place and each other.

With an open mind and some creativity, there are truly countless ways—big and small—to make our spaces feel like places where we, our loved ones, and guests truly belong together.

WHAT'S ABOVE YOUR HEAD & BELOW YOUR FEET AFFECTS HOW CONNECTIVE YOUR HOME FEELS

Whether you're bringing to life a new build or remodeling an older home, there's something about an intentional walk-through of the structure with your builder and designer that differs completely from looking at your plans on paper. It's the perfect time to consider the ways that your ceiling heights and flooring choices flow (or feel choppy and disconnected) as you move from room to room. Once again, the bigger-picture questions are worth asking: *How do the members of my household connect best and most often? What room feels most important for that kind of connection?*

On a recent walk-through with one of my clients, we revisited these questions. Originally she had wanted to make her foyer a dramatic moment complete with herringbone wood flooring. But as we moved through the spaces and talked about her and husband's passion for sharing good wine and hosting big dinners for friends (they are true foodies and brilliant cooks), I encouraged her to consider letting the dining room be the space that stood out as a special gathering point rather than putting the attention (via distinctive flooring) on the entryway. We ended up bringing limestone—part of their home's exterior makeup—into their dining-room design, cultivating a stronger tie-in with the story of the house itself and creating that wow factor in the space they are most excited about spending time together.

HOME STORY: #TWOEYESONDESIGNCLIENT

Helping a very dear friend, one who has worked on my KMI design team for many years, finish out her breathtaking abode, is one of the most delightful memories I have of creating a truly connective home atmosphere alongside someone. Not only does the layout of her home have a wonderfully easy flow from room to room but our kindred spirits and closeness as friends made the design process smooth and seamless because we ourselves are so connected. Drawing on my friend's Swedish heritage, we incorporated Nordic-inspired design touches throughout the home. And while staying true to that clean and airy style, we used materials with plenty of warmth and created lots of cozy spaces for Mom, Dad, and the three kids (one of whom is the most glorious and admirable bookworm I've ever known) to both tuck away and connect. Personal keepsakes (including a brass Greek goddess figurine, a thrift-store find my friend fell in love with—treasures come in all forms after all) earned prominent placement on display in the family room, ready reminders of the many stories—some of them still unfolding—that have made them who they are.

Cohesiveness between elements in a space—like these white oak–framed
cabinets, the white oak on the back of the kitchen island, and the color of
the woven counter stools—creates a clearer sense of place and welcome.

DON'T UNDERESTIMATE THE POWER
OF A GOOD CONVERSATION PIECE

Artwork—in all its limitless forms—continues to be one of the easiest ways to connect people
through conversation. It's just human nature to be drawn to something interesting, inspiring, or
even a bit strange on display in a home and want to know more about it. We can't help but ask,
"Is there a story behind this piece?" And, voilà, a conversation has begun, and we leave it knowing a little more about our host and feeling a little more connected to their home.

Certain types of furniture claim their own spin on being great "conversation pieces" by bringing people together literally. I love to incorporate a pair of swivel chairs into almost any family
room, sitting room, or sunroom. I mean, first of all, who doesn't love to swivel? And not only do
they cut a classy profile but the ability to swing effortlessly from a window view on one side and
then right into a good conversation on the other makes them attractive and highly functional at
the same time. Similarly, choosing a sofa with a bench cushion—one that runs the length of the
couch—offers a beautiful, seamless look while feeling more connective to those seated, rather
than an option with multiple, divided cushions. And really, if you end up being the one who
has to sit on the sofa crease, it kind of makes you feel like you're the extra or the overflow in the
space—the opposite of a sense of belonging, am I right?

I don't keep many sentimental pieces, but the charcoal cabinet pictured here has come with me to every move my husband and I have ever made. As the first piece of furniture we ever bought and painted together, it will always have a special place in whatever house we make our home.

OPPOSITE: For our client who dearly loves and misses her grandmother, we turned her grandmother's old sheet music into pieces of art that grace a cozy sitting nook, the perfect place to tuck in and be reminded of who you love and what is good.

SENTIMENTAL PIECES
CONNECT US TO OUR HOMES & EACH OTHER

Sometimes a sentimental piece, family heirloom, or historical artifact is either so striking in appearance or so important to us (or both) that it calls for the given space to be designed around it. Maybe it informs a color palette, lends to or lessens the formality of the room, introduces a pattern or texture, or deserves to be illuminated by its own art light. Other times, slipping a special memento onto a mantel, sideboard, built-in shelf, or the guest bedroom wall feels right—places where it can be rediscovered and enjoyed in subtler ways. It never fails to thrill me when I'm introduced to a piece, large or small, that is truly near and dear to my client's heart because it's always as unique as they are. I'm certain the same is true for you and the pieces you cherish most. A piano that has been passed down for generations, a drawing sketched by someone close to you, a vintage rug, written letters or journals, old maps, portraits, photos, collections from travel, artwork, and more—whatever the cherished item may be, one thing's for sure: highlighting that tangible treasure is a powerful way to weave the stories that make you *you* into the fabric of your home.

A little note to keep in mind when it comes to designing with sentimental pieces

Resist the urge to try to assign emotional significance to every decorative item in a space. Forcing meaning takes away from the authenticity of what you're creating. (If everything is special, nothing really is.) Let the items that are truly significant be just that and embrace the freedom to design with things that simply speak to your style or for no other reason than they're just really cool.

I have a painting that my maternal grandmother made a long time ago. It's a scene of a little country house surrounded by foliage. It's sweet but maybe not particularly stylish or noteworthy to someone unfamiliar with its origin. Still, I gladly hung the painting in a prominent spot in my guest bedroom, right above the bed, because that room is where my mom stays when she comes to visit me. Hanging her mother's painting there is my little way of saying "I love you, Mom." It gives her a meaningful way to connect my home, a way to know that she belongs here too.

PHOTOGRAPHY CREDITS

Erin Konrath: Cover, 6, 9, 12, 14, 15, 16, 17, 19, 21, 22–23, 24, 27, 79

Kevin Penczak: 156, 178, 179

Margaret Frances: 66

Margaret Rajic: 2, 32, 37 top, 37 bottom, 39, 40, 41, 42–43, 44, 45 top left, 45 bottom left, 45 bottom right, 48 left, 48 middle, 49 right, 50, 51, 64, 67, 69, 72–73, 78, 82, 83, 84–85, 87, 89, 90, 91, 92, 93 top, 93 bottom, 94, 95, 96 top left, 96 top right, 96 bottom left, 96 bottom right, 97, 113 top left, 138, 143 top, 143 bottom, 144, 145, 146, 147, 148, 150–51, 152 left, 152 middle, 153 right, 160, 162, 163 top, 163 bottom, 164, 165, 167, 169, 170–71, 176, 202, 216, 217

Maria Ponce Berre: 223

Stacy Markow: 18, 62

Stoffer Photography Interiors: 4, 28, 29, 30–31, 34, 35, 36, 38, 45 top right, 46–47, 53 bottom, 54, 57, 58, 59, 60, 61 top, 61 bottom, 68, 70 left, 70 middle, 71 right, 74, 75, 76, 80–81, 100, 102, 103, 104, 105, 107, 108, 109, 110–11, 113 top right, 113 bottom left, 113 bottom right, 114, 116, 117, 118, 119 top, 119 bottom, 120, 121, 122, 123, 124, 125, 126 left, 126 middle, 127 right, 128–29, 130, 131, 132, 133, 134, 136, 137, 140, 141, 149, 154, 155, 166, 172, 173, 174 left, 174 middle, 175 right, 177, 180, 182, 183, 184, 185, 186, 187, 188, 189, 190, 191, 192 left, 192 right, 193, 194, 197, 198, 199, 200, 201, 205, 206–7, 208, 209, 210, 211, 212, 213, 214, 215, 218–19, 220–21

ACKNOWLEDGMENTS

I extend my deepest gratitude to the people whose support, guidance, and encouragement have been indispensable in bringing this book to life. Charis Dietz, Brooke Rosolino, and the publishing team at Gibbs Smith have played pivotal roles, elevating the content, providing wisdom, and realizing the vision of this project.

Photographers, your talent in capturing the beauty and essence of the spaces I designed is truly remarkable. Your contributions have added depth and richness to this project.

To my clients: your trust, collaboration, and vision have been invaluable; and it's been an honor to bring your vision to life.

Builders and architects: your dedication and expertise have been instrumental; it's been such a rewarding collaboration. A special thanks goes to the KMI design team— your hard work and energy are reflected in every page of this book.

My appreciation extends to my parents, siblings, husband Ken, and daughters Lily and Myla for your love and inspiration, reminding me of the true meaning of "the love of home."

I attribute all blessings to the grace of the Lord. Without the contributions of each individual mentioned, this book would not have been possible.

With thanks,

Kate

ABOUT THE AUTHOR

From the heart of the Midwest, Kate Marker has spent over two decades refining her signature fresh and timeless style, cultivating a portfolio that now extends across the country. Guided by a design philosophy centered on creating spaces that exude warmth, comfort, and a deep connection to nature, Kate believes in crafting interiors that serve as sanctuaries—places where people instantly feel at ease and welcomed.

With a passion for designing spaces where one can linger and unwind, Kate's dedication to design has expanded beyond residential interiors to include an e-commerce site, a showroom, and collaborations with home brands that mirror her curated aesthetic.

In all her projects, Kate prioritizes comfort, ensuring that each piece of furniture and design element is not only visually pleasing but also practical and inviting. Plush textiles, cozy seating, and thoughtful layouts are hallmarks of her design approach, complemented by the incorporation of natural elements like wood, stone, and greenery.

By infusing her designs with the beauty of the outdoors, Kate believes in enhancing both visual appeal and a sense of tranquility and balance within a space. Above all, her goal is to create environments that authentically reflect the unique personality and lifestyle of each client, seamlessly blending her love for natural elements with a commitment to comfort to craft spaces that feel like true extensions of those who inhabit them.

Kate resides in the Chicago area with her husband and two daughters. When she's not immersed in her role as owner and principal designer, she finds solace and inspiration in weekend getaways to the family lake cottage in Michigan, and cultivates a sense of peace and perspective through yoga classes with friends.

FIRST EDITION
28 27 26 25 24   5 4 3 2

Text © 2024 Kate Marker

Published by
Gibbs Smith
570 N. Sportsplex Dr.
Kaysville, Utah 84037

1.800.835.4993 orders
www.gibbs-smith.com

Cover designer: Ryan Thomann
Interior designer: Virginia Snow
Art director: Ryan Thomann
Editor: Juree Sondker
Production manager: Felix Gregorio

Printed and bound in China

Library of Congress Control Number: 2024931124

ISBN 978-1-4236-6520-5

This product is made of FSC®-certified and other controlled material.